Bill Cosby

READ

Bill Cosby
and friends
for America's
Libraries

JUNIOR ■ WORLD ■ BIOGRAPHIES

Bill Cosby

Bruce W. Conord

CHELSEA JUNIORS 🌿

a division of CHELSEA HOUSE PUBLISHERS

Chelsea House Publishers

EDITOR-IN-CHIEF   Richard S. Papale
MANAGING EDITOR   Karyn Gullen Browne
COPY CHIEF   Philip Koslow
PICTURE EDITOR   Adrian G. Allen
ART DIRECTOR   Nora Wertz
MANUFACTURING DIRECTOR   Gerald Levine
SYSTEMS MANAGER   Lindsey Ottman
PRODUCTION COORDINATOR   Marie Claire Cebrián-Ume

JUNIOR WORLD BIOGRAPHIES

SENIOR EDITOR   Kathy Kuhtz

Staff for BILL COSBY
ASSOCIATE EDITOR   Terrance Dolan
COPY EDITOR   David Carter
EDITORIAL ASSISTANT   Robert Kimball Green
PICTURE RESEARCHER   Alan Gottlieb
SENIOR DESIGNER   Marjorie Zaum
COVER ILLUSTRATION   Bradford Brown

3 5 7 9 8 6 4 2

Library of Congress Cataloging-in-Publication Data
Conord, Bruce W.
    Bill Cosby/Bruce W. Conord
    p. cm.—(Junior world biographies)
    Includes index.
Summary: A biography of the popular entertainer, discussing his childhood, television shows, and continued success.
ISBN 0-7910-1761-3
      0-7910-1958-6 (pbk.)
1. Cosby, Bill, 1937– —Juvenile literature. 2. Entertainers—United States—Biography—Juvenile literature. 3. Comedians—United States—Biography—Juvenile literature. [1. Cosby, Bill, 1937– . 2. Entertainers. 3. Afro-Americans—Biography.] I. Title. II. Series.
PN2287.C632C6 1992   91-31711
792.7'028'092—dc20   CIP
[B]   AC

Contents

Comedian Bill Cosby, wearing a Fat Albert T-Shirt, clowns around on a tricycle in 1972. Cosby has never forgotten what it is like to be young.

Bill Cosby

Neighborhood children gather in front of the Richard Allen Homes in Philadelphia. Bill Cosby grew up in this low-income housing project.

1

"Happy To Be Alive"

Things were not going well for Malcolm Jamal Warner. He was very nervous, and he had just made a big mistake. The young actor was trying out for the part of Theo Huxtable on "The Cosby Show." The Theo Huxtable character was the 13-year-old son of Dr. Heathcliff Huxtable, played by Bill Cosby. At one point during the *audition*, Malcolm made a disgusted face when Dr. Huxtable spoke to him. By making a face, Malcolm hoped to get a laugh from the audience.

But Cosby was very unhappy about this. He did not want another show where the laughs came from making fun of other people, especially if it was a son making fun of his father. There were enough of those kinds of programs on television already.

The cameras stopped filming, and Cosby took Malcolm aside. He spoke quietly but firmly. "This show is about the love of a husband for his wife," Cosby explained. "It is about children who . . . respect their parents and can learn."

Malcolm Jamal Warner got the point. And he got the job. He was still nervous about working with such a big star, but Bill Cosby went out of his way to make Jamal and all the other cast members feel comfortable. Malcolm described his television dad as kind yet tough, and always funny. "When I am finally a father," Malcolm said, "I would like to copy his style. . . . You can talk to him whether you are eight or eighty." Young people especially have always found it easy to talk to Bill Cosby.

This is because Bill Cosby has always remembered what it was like to be young.

Bill Cosby was born on July 12, 1937, in Philadelphia, Pennsylvania. He was the oldest of four boys. His brothers' names were James, Russell, and Robert. Bill's mother, Anna Pearl, and his father, William Cosby, were childhood sweethearts from Virginia. After they got married, they moved to Philadelphia to build a better life. At first, William Cosby made enough money as a welder to comfortably support his little family. But as the family grew, William Cosby found it harder and harder to earn enough money to support them. He began to drink and to spend time away from home. Soon the Cosby family had to move to a cheaper apartment. They packed their things and moved into a tiny apartment in a poor section of North Philadelphia known as the Jungle.

Hard times had arrived for the Cosby family. Bill's father was drinking more and more. Often he disappeared for days and even weeks. One year, he vanished right before Christmas without leaving his family a cent. Christmas Eve arrived, but there was no Christmas tree or presents in the Cosby apartment. There were not even any stockings. "We didn't have enough socks for our feet," Bill remembered, "let alone any spare ones to hang."

Then tragedy made the hard times even harder. Bill was very close to his brother James, who was two years younger than Bill. They even shared the same bed. James seemed to get sick a lot. When he was six years old, he became very ill and died. Bill was heartbroken. Then things got even worse for the Cosby family. Bill's father went away and joined the navy. At first, he sent his paychecks home to his family. But eventually, the checks stopped coming. William Cosby was gone for good. Bill Cosby, age eight, was now the man of the house.

Bill's mother worked 12 hours a day as a maid in order to feed and clothe her children. Bill pitched in by shining shoes with a shoeshine stand he made from a wooden box. When he turned 11, he got a summer job at a local grocery store, working from six o'clock in the morning to six o'clock at night, for eight dollars a week.

Despite the hardships the family faced, the Cosby home was never a place of sadness or gloom. Bill and his mother made sure of that. Anna Pearl Cosby was a devoted and loving mother. Her strength and her love for her children helped smooth over the rough edges of poverty. Every night she tucked Bill and his brothers into bed and read aloud to them. She read stories by Mark Twain and Jonathan Swift, fairy tales from the brothers Grimm, and the Bible. She and Bill enjoyed Mark Twain's stories the most because they were funny. Like her oldest son, Anna Pearl Cosby had a strong sense of humor.

Bill was often the subject of his mother's humor. "She would tell me," Bill Cosby remembered years later, "that if I swallowed the seeds along with the grapes, branches would grow out of my ears and the neighbors would hang laundry on them. She would warn me that if I kept playing with my navel, it was going to pop out and all of the air would spew out of my body and I would fly around backwards, flopping around the room." Bill started carrying Band-Aids in his pockets, just in case his navel might pop.

It did not take young Bill Cosby long to develop his own sense of humor. By the time he was three or four years old, he had realized he could charm his mother out of a cookie by making her laugh. "That is how I started out to be a comedian," he later came to believe. Bill also used humor to offset the problems and disappointments of day-to-day life. "Bill could turn painful situations around and make them funny," remembered his brother Robert. "You laughed to keep from crying." One morning, when Bill's mother had to leave early for work, Bill volunteered to make breakfast for his hungry brothers. He added food coloring to their food, and his brothers were forced to eat purple waffles and green scrambled eggs.

Radio and television comedy also helped Bill keep an upbeat outlook on life. He enjoyed listening to the radio mystery and adventure programs that were popular during the 1940s. Radio series such as "The Lone Ranger" and "The Shadow" appealed to his imagination. But he loved the comedy programs most of all. Comedians such as Jack Benny, Jimmy Durante, and Fred Allen were among his favorites. "When comedy was on," Cosby said, "I was just happy to be alive."

Bill Cosby wanted to be like the comedians he heard on the radio. They made him laugh and feel good, and he wanted to make others feel good in the same way. The Cosby family could not afford a television, but a friend of Bill's was lucky enough to get one. Bill spent a lot of time at his friend's house, watching comedy shows on television. He studied the comedians to find out what made them funny. He watched famous funnymen Sid Caesar and Carl Reiner and learned to imitate the way they told their jokes. Then he practiced telling jokes to his friends and family. Another of Bill's favorite comedians was Sam Levenson. Levenson had a fascinating comedy style. Instead of telling short jokes, called *one-liners*, Levenson told funny stories. Levenson's stories, called *anecdotes*, were usually about his family, his friends, and his life as a teacher. Bill began collecting his own anecdotes. If something funny happened at home, he would make it into a story to tell later on. If something humorous happened while he was out playing with his friends, it would give him material for another story, which he might tell to his mother and his brothers at dinner one night.

Bill's grandfather, Samuel Russell, also had a great influence on the way Bill handled comedy. Grandfather Russell was a great storyteller. What Bill liked about his grandfather's stories was that they made him laugh and taught him an important lesson at the same time. "He loved to tell stories that had some moral point about getting an education and working hard," Bill recalled, "but you would hardly notice [that he was teaching you a lesson] because he would be so funny." Maybe the most important lesson that Bill learned from his grandfather was that teaching and learning can be

Comedian Sam Levenson tells one of his humorous stories on television in 1956. Cosby admired Levenson's style of comedy and started to tell funny stories of his own.

fun. Years later, this lesson would help make Bill Cosby one of the most successful and influential comedians of all time. But during his school years, it was a lesson he forgot all too often.

There was no question that Bill was very intelligent. But his report cards did not reflect this. Instead, they showed that he did not apply his intelligence to his schoolwork. Bill was more interested in being the class clown. "William would rather be a clown than a student and feels it is his mission to amuse classmates," one of his teachers wrote on his report card. Bill was a master of excuses and humorous reasons why he did not do his homework. All of his clowning and joking might have made him popular with the other students, but jokes could not win him good grades. By the time Bill reached sixth grade, he was in a class for difficult children at the Wister Elementary School. There he met a teacher named Mary Forchic. Bill's new teacher made a big impression on him. Mary Forchic was a dedicated teacher who believed that her students were basically good. She believed that they could be reached with hard work, patience, love, and understanding. She always rewarded her students for their efforts. Usually the students responded to her.

Mary Forchic saw that Bill Cosby was someone special. She wanted to bring out his unique qualities. In her opinion, "Every child is interested in something. The teacher's job is to find out what that something is. If it is baseball or football, for example, you can build math around that." Bill's interest turned out to be performing. So his teacher encouraged him to participate in school plays. Bill got his first taste of the spotlight, and he loved it. "Those classroom shows," he remembered, "were the things that generated the spark that said, 'Hey man, show business feels good!'"

Bill Cosby on the campus of Temple University in Philadelphia. Cosby enrolled at Temple in 1961 after serving in the U.S. Navy.

CHAPTER

2

Shorty
Grows Up

Mary Forchic opened up new doors for young Bill Cosby. She made him work hard, but she also made schoolwork fun for him. And she always applauded his efforts and made him feel good about his accomplishments. The first time he ever left his *inner-city* neighborhood was when she treated him to a movie. "I was so happy to be downtown," he recalled. "After the movie, my teacher took me to dinner and then she rode me home in a taxicab." Riding in a cab was a big deal in Bill's neighborhood. It meant that either something very bad or something very good had happened. For Bill, something very good had happened. Soon his grades improved greatly. He would never forget Mary Forchic. Her influence on his thoughts and his actions would eventually lead him to become a kind of teacher himself.

In the meantime, there was a lot more schooling to get through. And unfortunately for Bill, Mary Forchic could not follow him into junior high school and then high school. Without her to guide him, he slipped back into his old habits. In junior high school, his grades fell again. "I refused to accept the responsibility," he later admitted.

Despite his poor grades in junior high school, Bill scored very high on an intelligence test. This allowed him to attend Central High, the best public high school in Philadelphia. By this time, he was no longer little Bill Cosby. (He had been so small that his neighborhood friends had called him

Shorty.) Now he was a solid six-footer and a strong, speedy, talented athlete. As soon as he could, he joined Central High's football team. But in the first week of practice, he broke his arm. Without a team to be a part of, Bill felt lost and lonely in his new school. Most of the students at Central High were white, and they did not accept a poor black kid from the ghetto. Trying to make friends, Bill clowned and joked in class. It was not long before he was failing again.

Finally, Bill transferred to Germantown High School in North Philadelphia, where all his neighborhood friends went. There he had instant success, with his friends, with sports, and with girls. But not with his grades, which continued to fall. He was twice left back in the 10th grade. His junior year was his last at Germantown High. He was too old to compete in city track meets. If he could not play sports, he saw no sense in staying in school. In 1956, Bill dropped out of high school. He got a job as a shoemaker's helper, but he was quickly fired. His boss did not think it was funny when Bill nailed high heels from ladies' shoes to the bottoms of men's shoes.

Bill went from one low-paying job to another. He never stayed at one job for very long. Discouraged, he decided to follow his father's example and join the U.S. Navy. The navy was an eye-opening experience. At age 19, Bill finally found himself in a situation he could not joke his way out of. "For the first time," he recalled, "I was not able to argue or make an excuse for why I did not do something."

Cosby spent four hard years in the navy. It was an unpleasant experience, but he learned to make the best of it. In many ways, it matured him. During those four years, Cosby was trained as a *physical therapist*. His job was to help *rehabilitate* American soldiers who had been badly injured in the *Korean War*. Working every day with men who had lost their arms or legs, Cosby realized just how lucky he was. Never again would he feel sorry for himself because of the bad breaks he had received.

Cosby's years in the navy also changed his attitude about learning. "I was meeting navy men who really worked at bettering themselves," he said. "They were having difficulty with courses that I could do after reading them through once." He compared how little he had worked in school with how hard these men struggled to learn. He realized that it was wrong not to use his intelligence. "I was committing a sin—a mental sin," he decided. And he had wasted too much time already. Determined to become a high school graduate, Cosby enrolled in a *correspondence course*. By the time his four years in the navy were up, he had earned his high school diploma.

Cosby came out of the navy at the age of 22 with a new diploma and a new attitude. Now he was determined to go to college. He did not have nearly enough money to afford college, but he did have something that was as good as money.

Gavin White, the track and football coach at Temple University. White was impressed by Cosby's athletic abilities, his intelligence, and his sense of humor.

During his years in the navy, Cosby had continued to grow and improve as an athlete. He had made quite a name for himself as a member of the navy track-and-field team. He was swift, strong, and agile. He took his diploma and his reputation as an athlete and presented them to Gavin White, the football and track coach at Temple University in Philadelphia. Cosby also brought along his sense of humor. It did not take him long to win over Coach White. "We hit it off from the start," White remembered.

In 1961, Cosby was awarded an athletic *scholarship* to Temple University. He planned to study physical education. At Temple, Cosby applied himself to his studies. He maintained a B average. "I was reading, writing, challenging, exploring," he remembered. "I . . . had my act together." He also applied himself to track-and-field, basketball, and football. His best sport remained track-and-field, and he became the Middle Atlantic Conference high-jump champion.

Although he was serious about school, Cosby had not lost his sense of humor. He quickly earned a reputation as the track-and-field team joker. He kept his teammates in stitches by doing comic imitations of the coach's locker room pep talks. Sometimes Cosby brought his sense of humor to the playing field. Once, during a relay race, one of Cosby's teammates dropped the baton before he had a chance to pass it to Cosby. While Cosby waited impatiently, his teammate began to laugh. When he finally reached Cosby and handed him the baton, Cosby took it and bopped him on the head with it. Then he sprinted off to try and catch the other runners. At the end of the race, an exhausted Cosby fell down onto the track. His teammate, still laughing, came over, took the baton back, and bopped Cosby. The crowd loved it.

To earn spending money, Cosby worked at part-time jobs. During his sophomore year, he worked as a bartender in a local pub called the Underground. Naturally, Cosby tried to amuse his

A muscular Cosby clears the high-jump bar during track-and-field practice. Cosby was one of the best all-around athletes at Temple.

customers. He quickly learned that by making his customers laugh and have a good time he could earn larger tips. Soon, people were coming to the Underground just to hear the bartender's jokes and stories. Bill Cosby had his first real audience.

When it got to the point that he was doing more joke telling than drink making, the owners of the Underground hired Cosby to perform as a *stand-up comedian* in another one of their nightclubs, called the Cellar. The Cellar had no stage, and in order to be seen, Cosby had to perform on top of a table. But the ceiling was too low for him to stand. So, Cosby did some of his first stand-up comedy routines sitting down in a chair on top of a table.

Bill Cosby was making a name for himself as a Philadelphia comedian. He worked hard at comedy, studying the performances of successful comedians of the day, such as Mel Brooks, Lenny Bruce, Bob Newhart, and Jonathan Winters. During a break from school in the winter of 1962,

Cosby traveled to New York City to try out his act in bigger and better comedy clubs. He was good enough to land a job at the Gaslight, a popular New York City nightclub. The Gaslight paid Cosby $60 a week. This was big money to the young man from the North Philadelphia ghetto.

School started up again. Cosby's life grew more and more hectic. During the day, he attended classes and track-and-field practice at Temple. At night, he traveled to New York to perform at the Gaslight. While all this was going on, Cosby was also trying to decide what kind of comedian he wanted to be. He struggled to develop his own style of humor. Like many of the comedians of the early 1960s, Cosby told a lot of jokes about race relations in America. But he was not truly satisfied with racial humor. He did not feel that it was right to tell jokes about this controversial subject. "I do not think you can bring the races together by joking about the differences between them," Cosby insisted. Instead of racial humor, he began

Cosby performs one of his stand-up comedy routines. In 1962, Cosby left college to become a full-time entertainer.

to rely more on jokes and stories about everyday life, and about his family, friends, and boyhood days in North Philadelphia. As he told his stories, he made audiences feel like they were part of his family.

The audiences responded to the friendly Bill Cosby style. Cosby began to attract publicity. The *New York Times* reported that Cosby's act was "fresh" and "extremely funny." Cosby was now earning $175 a week at the Gaslight. At the end of the summer of 1962, he was hired to perform at the Gate of Horn in Chicago, for $200 a week. His career was taking off. But now he faced a difficult decision. He could no longer keep up with his studies and continue performing comedy at the same time. He had to choose between college and his comedy career. After agonizing over this situation, Cosby chose his career as an entertainer. He withdrew from Temple University. It was one of the hardest decisions he ever had to make.

Cosby and his wife, Camille, in a photograph taken in 1966. Cosby first met Camille in a bowling alley in Washington, D.C., and married her soon after.

3

"In My Own Way"

By 1963, Bill Cosby was making $500 a week for live performances. At the end of the year, he signed a contract with Warner Brothers record company to make a comedy album. The album was called *Bill Cosby Is a Very Funny Fellow . . . Right!* The album was a tremendous success. And while it was climbing the charts, very funny fellow Bill Cosby was falling in love.

Cosby first met the beautiful Camille Hanks at a bowling alley in Washington, D.C. Cosby was in Washington to perform in a nightclub called the Shadows. Camille was a 19-year-old *psychology* student at the University of Maryland. "The second week I knew him, he asked me to marry him," Camille recalled. "Three months later I said yes." But Camille's parents were not so sure about Cosby. They did not like the idea of their daughter marrying a comedian. Cosby was determined to win them over, however, and he did. On January 24, 1964, Cosby and Camille were married.

Cosby's career continued to soar. He was now getting $1,000 for a single live performance. In late 1964, he made the first of many appearances on Johnny Carson's "Tonight Show." Soon after, he released his second comedy album, called *I Started Out as a Child*. This album earned over $1 million in sales. It also earned Bill Cosby a *Grammy Award* for best comedy album of the year. More television appearances followed. He was invited to be the guest host on "The Tonight Show." (Since then, Cosby has appeared as "The Tonight Show" guest host more than 70 times.)

The cover of Bill Cosby's second comedy record album,
I Started Out as a Child. *Most of the stories on this*
popular album were about Cosby's childhood days
in Philadelphia.

Bill Cosby was becoming a familiar and welcome personality to millions of Americans.

One of the people who had noticed Cosby on television was *producer* Sheldon Leonard. In 1964, Leonard was planning a new television series for NBC. The series, called "I Spy," was about two American secret agents who had thrilling adventures around the world. Sheldon had chosen the actor Robert Culp to play one of the agents. After seeing Cosby on television, Leonard thought that he would be perfect for the role of the other agent. He offered the part to Cosby. Cosby took the job.

Leonard was taking a big chance in hiring Cosby for "I Spy." Cosby would be the first black American to have a major role in a popular television series. *Civil rights* and race relations were a big issue in America during the 1960s, and "I Spy" would be controversial. Before "I Spy," blacks had only been offered minor parts in movies and television shows. And these movies and shows always presented blacks as being inferior to whites. But in "I Spy," the black character played by Cosby and the white character played by Culp would be shown as equals. They would be good friends who helped each other out of dangerous situations. And Cosby's character would be just as smart, tough, and cool as Culp's character. Leonard and the NBC bosses were worried that white television viewers would not accept this. If the show failed, NBC would lose a lot of money. Cosby was worried too. There was a lot of pressure on him to succeed, not only for himself but for all black people in America.

Things did not go well at first. Cosby was obviously a great comedian, and he looked good on "The Tonight Show," but he had never really acted before. Cosby showed his nervousness and inexperience during the first "I Spy" rehearsals. His acting was not very good. He was stiff and unnatural in front of the cameras. He often stumbled over his lines. The NBC bosses wanted to fire him. But Robert Culp came to the rescue. Culp helped Cosby with his acting and made him feel relaxed. Like the characters they played on "I Spy," Culp and Cosby became fast friends. They liked and respected each other, and they worked well together. By the time the first episode of "I Spy" appeared on television, the NBC executives had stopped talking about firing Cosby.

"I Spy" was a smash hit. Audiences loved the Culp-Cosby teamwork and Cosby's cool sense of humor. "At 28," *Newsweek* magazine reported, "Cosby has accomplished in one year what scores of Negro actors and comedians have tried to do all their lives. He has completely [changed] the television image of the Negro." And there were no more doubts about Cosby's acting abilities. In 1966 he received an *Emmy Award* for best actor in a dramatic series. He received the same award for his work in "I Spy" in 1967 and 1968 as well.

Bill Cosby was a star. But all the attention

and money he was getting did not make him forget the more important things. He and his wife now had two daughters, Erika and Erinn, and he spent as much time as possible with his family, including his mother. One of the happiest moments in Cosby's life was when he walked into his mother's home and said to her, "You will never have to scrub any more floors or work in anybody else's house."

And Cosby had not forgotten Mary Forchic, the woman who had brought out the best in him back in grade school. He still dreamed of becoming a teacher and helping children, just as she had helped him. "I would like to become a teacher," Cosby said. "I think I have a talent for teaching; it is not so different from entertaining really, and if teaching's a thing you can do, it is something you *should* be doing." By 1969, Cosby was teaching. And he had the largest class in America. Anyone who tuned in to his new television series, "The Bill Cosby Show," was part of

Cosby and costar Robert Culp in a scene from the hit
television series "I Spy." Cosby was the first black actor
to star in a network television show.

Cosby's class. And every week, Cosby taught them a lesson in life.

"The Bill Cosby Show" was a lot different from "I Spy." There were no glamorous secret agents or dangerous situations on Cosby's new series. On "The Bill Cosby Show," he played a gym teacher named Chet Kincaid. Kincaid was not a spy or a detective; he was a regular guy. The new show was funny, but it was not a crazy comedy like so many other popular television shows. Nothing spectacular ever happened to Chet Kincaid. He lived a normal life, like most people. And like most people, he was not perfect. Cosby described his character as someone who "makes mistakes, and gets into trouble." Kincaid always learned a lesson from his mistakes, and Cosby hoped that his audience might learn the same lesson.

One episode of the "The Bill Cosby Show" was about the issue of *peer pressure* and the need for understanding between people of different religious backgrounds. In another episode, Kincaid tried to save a tree that was going to be chopped down to make way for a new building. And in one of the most memorable episodes, Kincaid tried to teach his football team that it was best to be humble in victory and gracious in defeat. But he did not practice what he preached. In a handball tournament, Kincaid tried a number of unfair tricks to win, only to lose to someone else who used the same poor sportsmanship. To make matters worse, Kincaid behaved like a poor loser as well. Chet Kincaid was a very human character.

Some people criticized Cosby's new show. They thought that Chet Kincaid was an unrealistic black character because he lived and behaved like *middle-class* white Americans. Because Bill Cosby was black, other blacks wanted him to confront racial issues on his shows, such as poverty and *discrimination*. This was not the first time Cosby had to defend himself against people who felt that his comedy should be more angry.

But Cosby believed in his own style of friendly comedy. He hoped that Chet Kincaid would appeal to most viewers simply as a human being and help both blacks and whites see that they had things in common. "I help black people in my own way," Cosby said. And he helped them in ways a lot of people did not know about. Behind the scenes, half the people who worked on "The Bill Cosby Show" were black. Many black actors were getting their first television roles on his program. And for the first time on American television, many episodes had all-black casts.

"The Bill Cosby Show" only lasted for two seasons. But by the time it went off the air, Cosby was involved in other projects. He continued to use television as a way to educate people, especially the young. In 1968, NBC presented a cartoon special called "Hey, Hey, Hey—It's Fat Albert." The show was about Cosby's colorful friends from his boyhood days in Philadelphia. Fat Albert and the other characters, such as Old Weird Harold, were so popular that NBC made the show a regular Saturday morning cartoon called "Fat Albert and the Cosby Kids." But Fat Albert and his friends were more than just funny. They were educational. Cosby said that they got "themselves involved in things like mathematical equations and what geometry is all about." Each episode had a lesson to teach, not only about things like math but about life in general.

Cosby continued to reach out to the young people in his audience. In 1971, he hosted a television special called "Bill Cosby Talks with Children About Drugs." He also made the first of many appearances on the exciting new public television series, "The Electric Company." "The Electric Company" was a show that helped children learn to read. Cosby's own children watched their father on "The Electric Company." By now, Cosby and Camille had a son, Ennis, in addition to their daughters, Erika and Erinn. (Cosby and his wife would eventually have two more daughters, Ensa and Evin. All those *E*'s, he explained, stood for *excellence*, something that Cosby hoped they would all achieve.)

Cosby's work with "The Electric Company" marked another turning point in his life. Cosby decided it was time to return to his own education. He moved his family from California to a 286-acre farm near Amherst, Massachusetts. Then, he enrolled at the nearby University of Massachusetts. He studied education. In spite of his hectic show business life, Cosby attended classes and studied hard. In 1972, he received a master's degree, and in May 1976, Cosby's lifelong dream came true. At age 38, he was awarded a doctorate in education. (In 1977, Cosby also earned his undergraduate degree in communications and theater from Temple University). His entire family and many of his friends were in the crowd watching him graduate. But it was Cosby's mother who seemed the most proud that day. "Mom just went crazy," Cosby said.

At the same time that he was earning a diploma at the University of Massachusetts, Cosby had started a new career as a movie star. His first movie, *Man and Boy*, was about a former slave struggling to support his family on a tiny farm. Cosby played Caleb, the former slave. As the movie opens, Caleb's plow horse is stolen, and he and his son set out to find it. They have quite a few adventures along the way. Although many people liked the movie, it did not do well at the box office. Neither did Cosby's second film, *Hickey and Boggs*, in which Cosby teamed up with Robert Culp from the old "I Spy" series.

Cosby's film career improved when he decided to act in a movie made by Sidney Poitier. Poitier was a black entertainer who had also broken racial barriers in American show business. (In 1964, Poitier became the first black to win an Oscar for best actor, for his performance in the movie *The Lilies of the Field*.) And like Cosby, Poitier did not appreciate the way blacks were

Cosby and actor Will Geer in an episode of "The Bill Cosby Show" filmed in 1970. In this series, Cosby played a gym teacher named Chet Kincaid.

being presented in American movies during the 1970s. Black characters were usually shown as as violent, angry people. Often they were drug dealers or other types of criminals. Poitier decided to make his own movies; they would be different from the standard black action films. Cosby, who was a friend of Poitier's, had similar ideas about movies. He agreed to act in Poitier's first movie, *Uptown Saturday Night*.

Uptown Saturday Night was a comedy about two friends, played by Poitier and Cosby, who try to track down a stolen lottery ticket. The movie was made for a family audience, and many families, both black and white, went to see it. *Uptown Saturday Night* became a huge success. Poitier and Cosby made two more movies that were similar in style to *Uptown Saturday Night*. *Let's Do It Again*, released in 1975, and *A Piece of the Action*, released in 1977, were both hits.

But after *A Piece of the Action*, Cosby's movie career began to go downhill. Most of the films he starred in during the late 1970s and early 1980s did not do well. During this period, his best film was *Bill Cosby, Himself*. It was a film of Cosby doing a live comedy show. Cosby performed while sitting in a chair, just as he had when he was first starting out as a comedian at the Underground nightclub in Philadelphia.

The Huxtable family. Standing, from left to right, are Tempestt Bledsoe (Vanessa), Malcolm Jamal Warner (Theo), and Phylicia Rashad (Clair). Seated, from left to right, are Lisa Bonet (Denise), Keshia Knight Pulliam (Rudy), Cosby, and Sabrina Le Beauf (Sondra).

4

An American
Family

By 1984, Bill Cosby was ready to return to
television. He had an idea for a new series. It would
be about the Huxtables, a black family. Cosby
would play the father, a doctor. He would have
five children, and his wife would be a lawyer. The
Huxtables would be a lot like Cosby's own family.
They would be wealthy and well educated. And
they would be a close, happy family.

Once again, the executives at NBC had
doubts. They believed that most Americans want-

ed to see silly comedies or violent action dramas. They wondered if America was ready for this kind of show. They wondered if Bill Cosby still had enough appeal. Most of them had no idea that "The Cosby Show" would become one of the most successful series in the history of television.

The idea for "The Cosby Show" came to Cosby late one night while he watched television. As he changed channels, he became disturbed by what he saw. There seemed to be so much sex, violence, and nastiness on television. "Television," Cosby had always believed, "should be something a family can look at and get a good feeling from." But he did not get a good feeling from what he saw. And Cosby did not like the idea of his own children watching all the gunfights and car crashes he saw on television.

Cosby began to think of ideas for a new television show. (Creating a program his children could watch, he joked, would be easier than throwing away the family's six television sets.)

His first idea was a detective show that would have no guns, violence, or even car chases. "I would solve crimes with my wits," he explained, "and my girl would be a strong woman with her own career." But the three major television *networks* did not like this idea. They felt that there were too many detective and police shows on the air already.

Finally, after talking it over with his wife, Cosby decided on a weekly *situation comedy* about a black family. This family would be different from most other black families shown on television because the mother and father would be extremely successful people. Cosby also wanted the show to be thoughtful and sensitive, like "The Bill Cosby Show." This was how the Huxtable family was born.

"The Cosby Show" began in the fall of 1984 on NBC. It was an instant success with television viewers of all ages. Cosby had read the public's mind correctly. Like Cosby, millions of viewers

Bill and Camille Cosby at the dedication of a renovated wing of a children's center in Boston. Cosby helped to raise funds for the center, and he continues to spend much of his time and money supporting worthwhile causes, especially education. In 1988, he and his wife donated $20 million to Spelman College in Atlanta.

wanted a wholesome family show that would entertain, amuse, and also make them think. "The Cosby Show" quickly became the top-rated show on television. It remained at or near the top of the ratings during its entire eight years on NBC.

"The Cosby Show" was about family life. The stories for many of the episodes came from Cosby's own experiences as a father. In one episode, Theo Huxtable, played by Malcolm Jamal Warner, worried that he had not received a good enough grade to please his father, even though he had studied very hard. But Theo soon learned that to his father, the effort was the most important thing. In real life, Bill Cosby had the same attitude, and he taught his children that trying hard was more important than getting an A on a test. In another episode, one of the Huxtable children blamed her father for causing trouble for her at school. Because the Huxtables were rich, the kids at school had been teasing her. "You are poor," Dr. Huxtable told her. "Your father is rich." It is easy to imagine Cosby making a humorous remark like that to one of his own children.

Viewers of "The Cosby Show" got a chance to look into Bill Cosby's private life. There were many similarities between the Cosby family and the Huxtable family. The Huxtable's New York home was a lot like the Cosby home near Amherst, Massachusetts. The Huxtables had five children who resembled the five Cosby children. (But they were not exactly alike. The real-life Cosby children met the Huxtable children one day at the Cosby home. Malcolm Jamal Warner was surprised to see that his *counterpart*, Ennis Cosby, was almost a foot taller than he was. Ennis won easily when they played basketball against each other.)

There were also important similarities between Camille Cosby and Mrs. Huxtable. Like Camille, Cosby's television wife was a well-educated, independent woman. Camille Cosby is a college graduate as well as a full-time mother. She even pilots an airplane. Sometimes, when she cannot find a chance to talk to her husband alone because of his busy schedule, she takes him up in her plane. "I am the only one who knows what is going on up here and there is something I would like to talk to you about," she then tells her husband. He has no choice but to listen. "It is not fair the way she uses that plane," he jokes.

Phylicia Rashad, the actress who plays Mrs. Huxtable, was thrilled to be chosen for the part. She believed that "The Cosby Show" characters were good *role models* for young black people. "Kids learn by example," she said, "and I think we are very good ones."

"The Cosby Show" was a huge success, but there were still people who thought that Bill Cosby was not doing the right thing as a black entertainer. They believed that he was creating an unrealistic picture of black life in America. They complained that Cosby was setting goals that were too high for most black children to reach. But Cosby believed that his show was realistic. There *were* successful black families in America. There were black families where the mother was a lawyer and the father was a doctor. "My point is," he said, "that this is an American family—an *American* family—and if you want to live like they do, and you are willing to work, the opportunity is here." Dr. Alvin Poussaint, a black professor at Harvard University, agreed with Cosby. He said that "The Cosby Show" presented blacks "as decent, productive human beings . . . and it cuts racial barriers by showing that we are all just people."

The character of Dr. Heathcliff Huxtable made Bill Cosby the most recognizable father in America. When people thought about Bill Cosby, they saw him as Dr. Huxtable. And when people thought about Dr. Huxtable, they thought about him as a father. Through Dr. Huxtable, Cosby was able to express his feelings about the importance of being a good father. Just about everyone who ever watched the show liked and admired Dr. Huxtable. He was not perfect, but he was smart, funny, patient, and understanding. Most of all, he was a good father.

In 1986, Cosby wrote a book about being a father. It was called *Fatherhood*. Cosby had written other humorous books, but this one was much more popular. *Fatherhood* was a collection of anecdotes and thoughts on being a dad. Because of his role as Dr. Huxtable, a lot of people, fathers especially, were interested in what he had to say. Almost 3 million hardcover copies of *Fatherhood* were sold.

After *Fatherhood*, Cosby wrote two more popular books. *Time Flies* was a book about growing older. It was published just in time for Cosby's 50th birthday. In 1989, Cosby published *Love and Marriage*, which was about marriage in general and Cosby's own marriage to Camille. Like *Fatherhood*, these two books were both humorous and thoughtful, and they proved once again that Bill Cosby was much more than just a joke teller.

In June 1991, to the surprise and disappointment of millions of television viewers, Cosby announced that "The Cosby Show" was ending.

Cosby and New York City mayor David Dinkins address students at Brooklyn's Thomas Jefferson High School in 1992. The mayor and Cosby asked the young people to reject violence in their school, where two students had recently been killed.

The show had come a long way after eight seasons, but Cosby wanted to move on to other things. Bill Cosby had also come a long way. The little boy who was once called Shorty was now a movie star, a famous comedian, a television star, a major producer, a teacher, and a best-selling author. He was also one of the richest entertainers in the world. Cosby and Camille felt lucky to be living such a good life, so they decided to give something back. They donated $20 million to Spelman College in Atlanta. It was the largest donation ever made to a black college.

Bill Cosby continues to do live comedy performances. He appears often on various television shows such as "The Tonight Show" and "Late Night with David Letterman." He is involved in promoting college athletics, and he is even working on a jazz album. He continues writing books. He also remains active in social issues that affect young people. Cosby has appeared at numerous schools to speak against drug use, gangs, and violence. Like many parents, he is concerned about the problems that today's children face. "Providing a good example for [children] is very important," he explained. "I love being around them, and I feel I gain as much from them as they hopefully learn from me."

Bill Cosby is also planning new television projects. One of these projects is a new version of "You Bet Your Life." "You Bet Your Life" was one of the most popular television shows of the 1950s. The star of the show was Groucho Marx. Groucho was one of the Marx Brothers, a famous team of comedians. (Groucho's brothers were Harpo, Chico, Zeppo, and Gummo.) Groucho was known for his big mustache, his goofy glasses, and his lightning-quick sense of humor.

As the host of "You Bet Your Life," Groucho would ask two contestants about themselves. He would continually make jokes while they tried to answer, keeping the studio audience in an uproar. Behind the contestants was a funny-looking fake duck that only the audience could see.

A card in the duck's mouth showed a secret word. If the contestants used the secret word in their answers to Groucho's questions, they won money. Bill Cosby's "You Bet Your Life" would be similar, with Cosby taking over Groucho's spot as host. Many people believe that Cosby is perfect for the role of the wisecracking game-show host.

Despite his wealth, his fame, and his busy schedule, Bill Cosby has never lost sight of what is most important to him in life. The education of young people is still his primary goal. As long as there are kids of all ages willing to learn about life, Bill Cosby is willing to teach them and to make them laugh at the same time.

In 1976, Cosby receives a doctorate in education from the University of Massachusetts in Amherst.

Further Reading

Other Biographies of Bill Cosby

Haskins, Jim. *Bill Cosby*. New York: Walker & Co., 1988.

Woods, Geraldine and Harold Woods. *Bill Cosby: Making America Laugh and Learn*. Minneapolis, MN: Dillon, 1983.

Selected Recordings

A House Full of Love: Music from the Bill Cosby Show. Columbia, 1986.

When I Was a Kid. MCA, 1971.

Chronology

July 12, 1937   Born William Henry Cosby, Jr., in Philadelphia, Pennsylvania

1956   Drops out of high school and joins the U.S. Navy; becomes a physical therapist

1959   Passes a high school equivalency exam

1960   Leaves the U.S. Navy

1961   Wins athletic scholarship and enrolls at Temple University

1962 Begins career as a stand-up comedian; leaves Temple University

1963 Records first comedy album, *Bill Cosby Is a Very Funny Fellow . . . Right!*

1964 Marries Camille Hanks; makes first appearance on "The Tonight Show"

1965 Serves for the first time as guest host on "The Tonight Show"; wins first Grammy Award (for *I Started Out as a Child);* debuts in "I Spy" and becomes the first black to star in a dramatic television series

1966 Wins first Emmy Award

1969 Debuts in "The Bill Cosby Show"

1972 Appears in first feature film, *Man and Boy*

1976 Receives a doctorate in education from the University of Massachusetts

1977 Receives a B.A. degree from Temple University

1983   Appears in film of his live stand-up act, *Bill Cosby, Himself*

1984   Debuts in "The Cosby Show"

1986   Publishes a best-seller, *Fatherhood*

1991   Announces that "The Cosby Show" is ending

1992   Visits Thomas Jefferson High School in Brooklyn, New York, on March 2 to plead for peace after two students were killed there

Glossary

anecdote   a short story about an interesting or amusing incident

audition   a short performance to test the ability of an actor

civil rights   the personal and property rights recognized by a government and guaranteed by its laws and constitution

correspondence course   a class in which the teacher instructs a student by mail, sending lessons and exams to the student

counterpart   a person or thing that is exactly or very much like another

discrimination   the unfair treatment of an individual, group, or race

Emmy Award   an award given for outstanding performances and productions in television

Grammy Award   an award given for outstanding achievement in the recording industry

inner city   the older, central part of a city, particularly the crowded, run-down, and poor neighborhoods found there

Korean War   a war fought between North Korea and South Korea from 1950 to 1953; the United Nations, which included the United States, fought on South Korea's side

middle class   the social and economic class between the rich and the poor

network   a group of related radio or television stations that share programs

one-liner   a very short, clever joke or comment

peer pressure   an attempt by a group of people to influence the behavior of a member of that group

physical therapist   a person who treats disease or injury by physical and mechanical means (massage, regulated exercise, water, light, heat, or electricity)

producer   a person who supervises and usually finances the making of a movie or television program

psychology   the study of the mind and human behavior

rehabilitate   to restore a person to a condition of health

role model   a person whose behavior is imitated by others

scholarship   money awarded to a student

situation comedy   a humorous radio or television series that involves a familiar cast of characters in a succession of episodes

stand-up comedian   a comedian who usually performs alone, standing up on a stage in front of a live audience

Index

74

Picture Credits

Courtesy of American Library Association: frontispiece; AP/Wide World Photos: pp. 6, 17, 32, 34, 49, 52, 62; Courtesy of News Office, University of Massachusetts at Amherst: p. 66; Courtesy of Temple University News Bureau: pp. 20, 26, 29; UPI/Bettmann: pp. 42, 56; Urban Archives, Temple University Libraries: p. 8

Bruce W. Conord is a graduate of Rutgers University and a freelance writer. His articles have appeared in several newspapers and magazines, including the *Trenton Times* and *American History Illustrated*. He is also the author of *Cesar Chavez* in the Chelsea House JUNIOR WORLD BIOGRAPHIES series. Mr. Conord lives in Hightstown, New Jersey, with his wife, two dogs, and a cat.